COMMUNITY HELPERS

Police Officers

BLASTOFF! READERS 1

by Christina Leaf

BELLWETHER MEDIA • MINNEAPOLIS, MN

Note to Librarians, Teachers, and Parents:

Blastoff! Readers are carefully developed by literacy experts and combine standards-based content with developmentally appropriate text.

Level 1 provides the most support through repetition of high-frequency words, light text, predictable sentence patterns, and strong visual support.

Level 2 offers early readers a bit more challenge through varied simple sentences, increased text load, and less repetition of high-frequency words.

Level 3 advances early-fluent readers toward fluency through increased text and concept load, less reliance on visuals, longer sentences, and more literary language.

Level 4 builds reading stamina by providing more text per page, increased use of punctuation, greater variation in sentence patterns, and increasingly challenging vocabulary.

Level 5 encourages children to move from "learning to read" to "reading to learn" by providing even more text, varied writing styles, and less familiar topics.

Whichever book is right for your reader, Blastoff! Readers are the perfect books to build confidence and encourage a love of reading that will last a lifetime!

This edition first published in 2018 by Bellwether Media, Inc.

Library of Congress Cataloging-in-Publication Data

Names: Leaf, Christina, author.
Title: Police Officers / by Christina Leaf.
Description: Minneapolis, MN : Bellwether Media, Inc., [2018] | Series: Blastoff! Readers: Community Helpers | Audience: Age: 5-8. | Audience: K to Grade 3. | Includes bibliographical references and index.
Identifiers: LCCN 2017032151 (print) | LCCN 2017039613 (ebook) | ISBN 9781626177499 (hardcover : alk. paper) | ISBN 9781681034508 (ebook) | ISBN 9781618913098 (pbk. : alk. paper)
Subjects: LCSH: Police–Juvenile literature.
Classification: LCC HV7922 (ebook) | LCC HV7922 .L4293 2018 (print) | DDC 363.2–dc23
LC record available at https://lccn.loc.gov/2017032151

Editor: Nathan Sommer Designer: Brittany McIntosh

Printed in the United States of America, North Mankato, MN.

Table of Contents

Car Chase!

Whoosh! A car speeds down the road. A police car races after it.

POLICE

More officers join the chase. Then the driver pulls over. He is under **arrest**!

What Are Police Officers?

Police officers keep communities safe. They make sure everybody follows the law.

POLICE
POLICE
eloitte.

Officers patrol roads and public places. **Police stations** are their bases.

POLICE

What Do Police Officers Do?

Police officers stop people who break the law. They give tickets and make arrests.

Officers work to catch **crimes** before they happen. They also study **crime scenes** and **suspects**.

Police Officer Gear

police car radio handcuffs flashlight

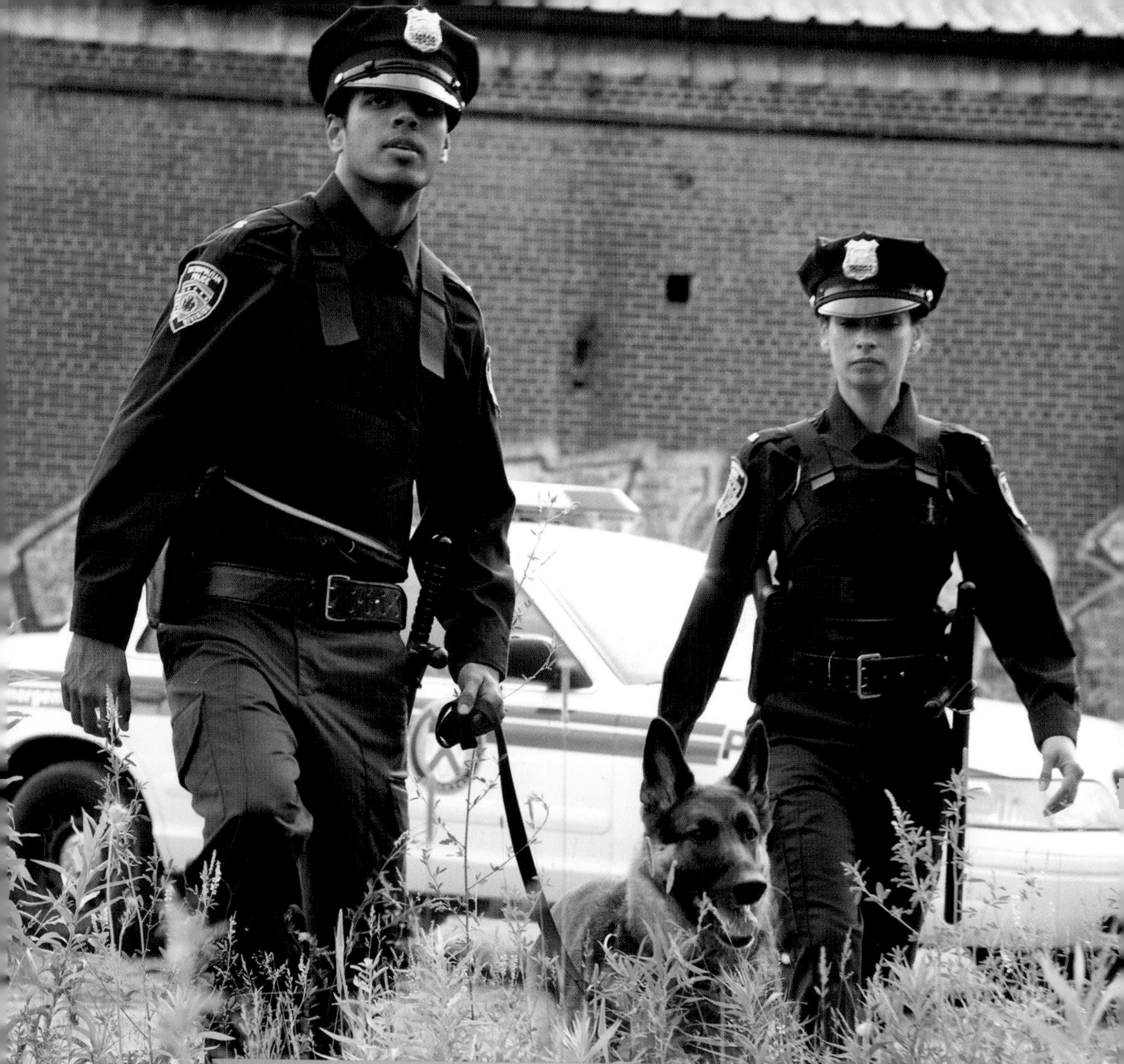

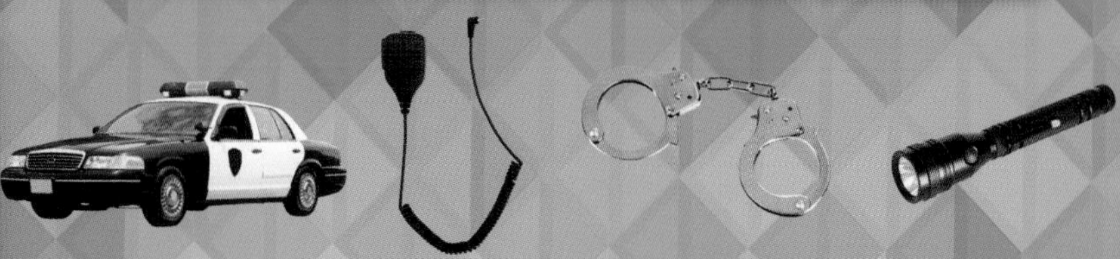

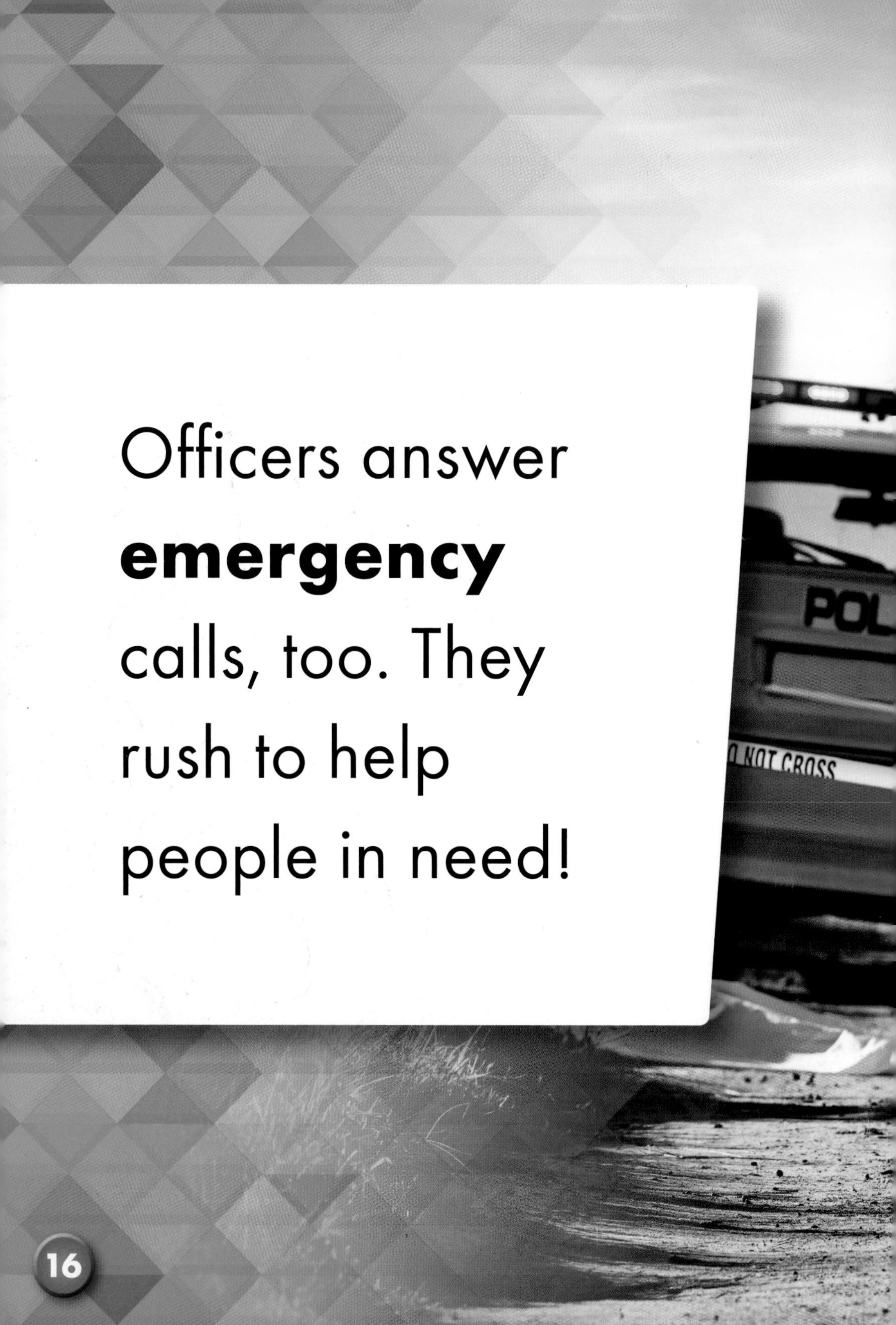

Officers answer **emergency** calls, too. They rush to help people in need!

POLICE
POLICE

What Makes a Good Police Officer?

Officers make tough choices each day. They must take the right action.

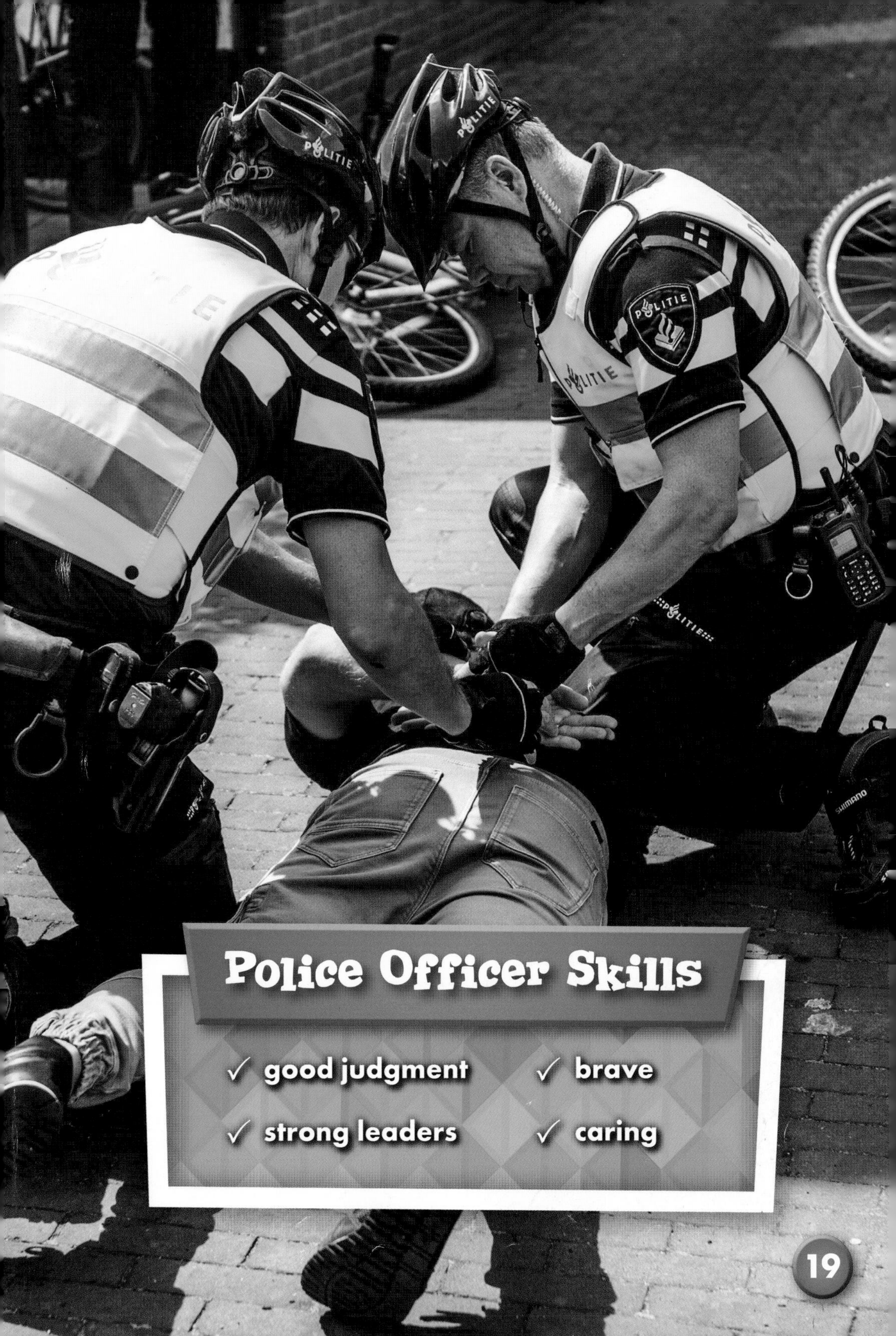

Police Officer Skills

- ✓ good judgment
- ✓ brave
- ✓ strong leaders
- ✓ caring

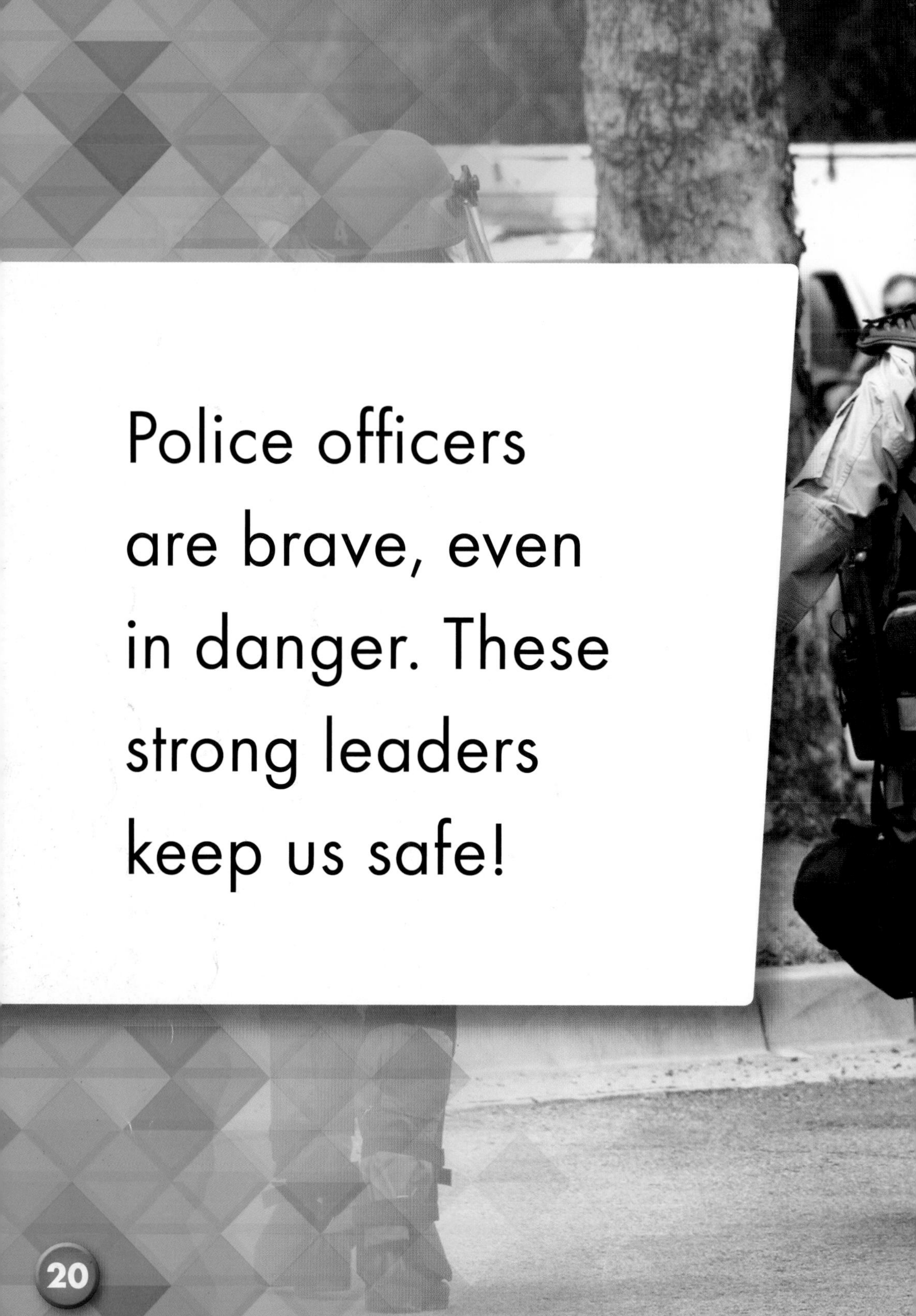

Police officers are brave, even in danger. These strong leaders keep us safe!

4
3
4
SHERIFF
SHERIFF

Glossary

arrest

in police control

emergency

an unexpected situation that calls for quick action

crime scenes

places where crimes took place

police stations

buildings where police officers work

crimes

actions that break the law

suspects

people who are believed to have broken the law

To Learn More

AT THE LIBRARY

Bluemel Oldfield, Dawn. *Police Dogs*. New York, N.Y.: Bearport Publishing, 2014.

Parkes, Elle. *Hooray for Police Officers!* Minneapolis, Minn.: Lerner Publications, 2017.

Spaight, Anne J. *Police Cars on the Go*. Minneapolis, Minn.: Lerner Publications, 2016.

ON THE WEB

Learning more about police officers is as easy as 1, 2, 3.

1. Go to www.factsurfer.com.
2. Enter "police officers" into the search box.
3. Click the "Surf" button and you will see a list of related web sites.

With factsurfer.com, finding more information is just a click away.

Index

The images in this book are reproduced through the courtesy of: Marmaduke St. John/ Alamy, front cover; stockelements, pp. 2-3; Adwo, p. 4-5; sirtravelalot, pp. 6-7, 22 (top left); arindambanerjee, pp. 8-9; Debu55y, pp. 10-11; kali9, pp. 12-13; Radius Images/ Alamy, pp. 14-15; travis manley, p. 15 (police car); Vladimir_ Zhukov, p. 15 (flashlight); Veronica Louro, p. 15 (handcuffs); Teamdaddy, p. 15 (radio); Yuri_Arcurs, pp. 16-17; Peter Braakmann, pp. 18-19; Darleine Heitman, pp. 20-21; Prath, p. 22 (center left); tommaso79, p. 22 (bottom left); OgnjenO, p. 22 (top right); Nils Versemann, p. 22 (center right); Lisa F. Young, p. 22 (bottom right).